Daily Blessings
for My
Wife

Daily Blessings for My Wife

ISBN 1-59027-038-X

Published by Popular Publishing Company, LLC
3 Park Avenue
New York, New York 10016

Developed by GRQ Ink, Inc.
Manuscript written by Christopher Douglas
Cover and text design by Richmond & Williams
Composition by Educational Publishing Concepts, Inc.

Daily Blessings
for My
Wife

THE
POPULAR
GROUP
New York, New York

How sweet is
your love,
my treasure,
my bride!

Song of Solomon 4:10 NLT

He who finds a wife finds a good thing,
And obtains favor from the LORD.

PROVERBS 18:22 NKJV

My Dear Wife,

I have so much to tell you.

I know I'm not always the best at putting deeply felt things into words, but I want you to know how much I love you, how much you mean to me, and how important our marriage is.

I chose this little book because it explains a lot of the things I think and feel when it comes to us, and our relationship. I hope that as you read it, you will know that these letters and prayers reflect my heart and my love for you.

I long to see us grow closer. I want to get better at sharing my feelings and listening to yours. I want our friendship to get stronger and our love to become a rock-solid foundation supporting a marriage that will last and last.

Because I love you,

Your Husband

I'll Love You Forever

Dear friends, let us love one another,
for love comes from God.
Everyone who loves has been born of God
and knows God.

1 JOHN 4:7 NIV

⌒◎⌒

*M*y Dear Wife,

My love for you is endless. I know I don't always show it, and I admit that I sometimes get distracted with the demands of life and the pressures of work. But I want you to know that my love for you is here to stay—it's going to go the distance. I am committed to you, and I'm committed to our marriage. I plan to love you for all of my days.

I'm aware that things don't always go smoothly in our marriage and that we have our ups and downs, but through it all, one thing will never change—my love for you. I know it will go on and on. And I know that it will continue to increase and strengthen over time. My love for you is forever.

⌒◎⌒

*D*ear God, remind us that love is more than a feeling—it is a commitment to hang in there through thick and thin. Help us as we daily choose to love like that—and enjoy what comes of it. Amen.

I Promise You

**For this reason a man shall leave his father and mother
and be joined to his wife,
and the two shall become one flesh.**

EPHESIANS 5:31 NKJV

My Dear Wife,

I bless you for honoring our vows. I remember the day, my love, when we repeated our wedding vows. I was nervous, my palms were sweaty, and I longed for the whole thing to hurry up and end. But at the same time, I wanted it to go on forever. You were so beautiful, my bride. I still remember the sparkle in your eyes as you walked down the aisle toward me. On that day, I promised, before God and the whole world, to love and to cherish you for the rest of your days.

I still stand by that promise—maybe even more now than I did then, for now I better understand the significance of such a vow. Here and now, I promise you that I will be committed to our marriage for the rest of my life. I love you.

Dear God, bless us as we reaffirm our promise to love and cherish each other for all of our days. Amen.

The First Time We Met

My darling, you are like a mare among the king's stallions.
Your cheeks are beautiful with ornaments,
and your neck with jewels.

SONG OF SOLOMON 1:9-10 NCV

❦

My Dear Wife,

You are still my lovely one. I remember the first time I saw your face, that bright, cheery smile, those sparkling eyes. It was all over—I was smitten. Maybe I didn't quite know what hit me at first, or maybe I was afraid to admit that it could actually happen to me. But it was indisputable; I was hooked. I'm so thankful I was.

I remember the first time we talked. I had difficulty concentrating on your words because it was all I could do to resist reaching out and touching your hair, your cheek, your lips. I remember that little twinkle in your eye, that teasing smile-as if you knew that it was only a matter of time. I thank God for that day.

❦

Dear God, help us never to forget those first moments we spent together. Thank You for causing our two separate lives to gently collide and become so beautifully one. Amen.

When You Were a Little Girl

*When I was a child, I spoke as a child, I understood as a child, I
thought as a child; but when I became a man,
I put away childish things.*

1 CORINTHIANS 13:11 NKJV

My Dear Wife,

I love the little girl in you. I wish I'd known you as a small child. I bet
you were smart and funny. I bet you knew how to climb trees, and I
wonder if you had tea parties. Would you have invited me? And I have so
many other questions: Did you play with dolls? Did you roller-skate? Did
you ever fall down and skin your knee? Or break a bone? I wish I could
go back in time, help you up, and make it all better. We probably would've
been good friends, you and I.

Tell me what you were like as a child. What were your grandest dreams
and worst fears? What was your happiest time? Did anyone ever hurt you?
Were you ever lonely? I want to know all there is to know about you—
please, don't hesitate to tell me.

Dear God, there are so many things in our lives that make us who we
are today. Help us as we get to know each other in new ways. Amen.

Let's Grow Old Together

The righteous will flourish like a palm tree, . . .
they will flourish in the courts of our God.
They will still bear fruit in old age,
they will stay fresh and green.

PSALM 92:12-14 NIV

*M*y Dear Wife,

You grow more beautiful with time. Can you imagine the two of us with gray hair and lots of wrinkles—with steps that move slowly and ears that have grown faint of hearing? It's difficult to imagine, but there is no stopping the clock. You'll look cute when your hair turns white, and my love for you will see past the wrinkled exterior to the you inside.

Let's not fight aging. Instead, let's accept that it happens and rejoice in the number of years we share together. The more I am with you, my darling, the more deeply I fall in love with you. Our love will sweeten and mellow with the passing of time.

---

*D*ear God, thank You for the gift of a companion with whom to grow old. That is a blessing from You. Help us to keep our love strong and vibrant as the years go by. Amen.

I Love Your Face

Ah, you are beautiful, my love; ah, you are beautiful;
your eyes are doves.
Ah, you are beautiful, my beloved,
truly lovely.

SONG OF SOLOMON 1:15-16 NRSV

My Dear Wife,

Your countenance is my blessing. Do you know how much I love to look at your face? I enjoy it most when you don't know I'm looking. I love the curve of your cheek, the shape of your chin, the form of your lips. I love the color of your eyes and the way your lashes flutter softly, like butterflies. I love the way your brows lift and your mouth puckers slightly when you're considering something.

I love to touch your face, to feel the smoothness of your skin beneath my hands. I love to run my fingers over your closed eyelids, down your neck, over your lips. Oh, darling, how I love your face.

Dear God, thank You for the little things that bring so much pleasure to our lives—the joy of a familiar expression, the gentle touch of a fingertip. Remind us to express our love for each other every day. Amen.

I Need Someone to Talk To

Telling the truth in love, we should grow up in every way toward Him who is the Head—Christ.

EPHESIANS 4:15 MLB

‿ᗤᗧᗤ‿

My Dear Wife,

I bless you for listening. I know that sometimes I might act as if I'm self-sufficient, as if I don't need anyone or anything. But beneath my I-have-everything-under-control exterior dwells a needy little boy with concerns, insecurities, and a need to be heard. Even when I appear quiet and withdrawn, sometimes I just want someone to talk to. If you can gently nudge me out, I'd love to talk to you.

Communication seems to flow more easily for you women than it does for us men. We're not always comfortable saying how we feel—or even knowing how we feel. But you can draw me out. I know you're a good listener, and you usually have something wise and encouraging to say. And I really do need to talk.

‿ᗤᗧᗤ‿

Dear God, help me to become a better communicator. And help us to know when it's time to talk. Show us ways to share what's going on inside us. Teach us to be good listeners. Amen.

Trust Me

**It is God who is at work in you,
enabling you both to will and to work
for his good pleasure.**

PHILIPPIANS 2:13 NRSV

ன௫௸

*M*y Dear Wife,

I love how you trust me. One of the toughest issues in marriage has to do with the area of trust. At the same time, I know that trust is critical to a good relationship. I realize that trust doesn't just happen; it is built—one brick at a time—like a foundation. It would mean so much to me to know that you really trust me.

I'm not perfect. I know I've let you down from time to time. But I want you to know that I'm willing to work hard to assure you that your life is completely safe in my hands. I take that seriously, and I pray that God will help me make good on that promise.

ன௫௸

*D*ear God, please help us to build a strong foundation of trust in our marriage. Only You can make us into people who are truly trustworthy. We come to You now and ask for Your touch in our lives. Amen.

I Forgive You

Be kind toward one another, tenderhearted,
forgiving one another, even as God
has in Christ forgiven you.

EPHESIANS 4:32 MLB

My Dear Wife,

You are so easy to forgive. Little irritations—small offenses, emotional wounds, hurt feelings—build up over time. Sometimes they are temporarily overlooked, buried, or nearly forgotten—but not quite. I've been responsible for my share of hurts, and for that I'm truly sorry. Please forgive me. I also want to make sure that I've forgiven you. I don't want to carry around an old offense that breeds bitterness and eventually pushes us apart.

A vital part of any loving and lasting relationship must be forgiveness. We cannot survive without it. It's impossible to love someone without inflicting hurt from time to time. We're human, and we're imperfect at this thing called love. So let's continue to choose to forgive.

Dear God, we choose not to carry offenses against each other. Remind us when pass through the irritations of everyday life to freely forgive and to receive forgiveness. Amen.

We Don't Always Agree

Blessed are the peacemakers,
for they will be called children of God.

MATTHEW 5:9 NRSV

ର୍ତ୍ତ

My Dear Wife,

Bless you for speaking your mind. We don't always agree on every issue, but that only means we each have a mind of our own. And that makes life a lot more interesting. We know, too, that sometimes there can be more than one right answer or more than one right way of doing something. Sometimes the best answers come from approaching problems from different angles. One person wisely said, "If we always agreed on everything, then one of us would be unnecessary." And we're both very necessary.

So, dear one, let's agree to disagree. Let's do it in peace. Let's welcome some lively discussions, enjoy a good debate, and practice active listening skills. I know there is much I can learn from you. So I promise to be respectful of your philosophies and ideals. In the same way, I hope you'll respect mine. After all, two heads are better than one.

───────────── ର୍ତ୍ତ ─────────────

Dear God, teach each of us to respect and value the other's opinion, even when it differs from our own. Amen.

I Forget to Ask

*Rejoice. Change your ways. Encourage each other. Live in
harmony and peace. Then the God of love and peace
will be with you.*

2 CORINTHIANS 13:11 NLT

⊱◦◦⊰

My Dear Wife,

I love how you remind me. I admit that sometimes I get so caught up in
my own world, my own work, and my own responsibilities that I forget to
inquire about how you're doing. Please forgive me. It's not that I don't care.
Or even that I don't want to hear. It's just that I get preoccupied and
neglect what's really important to me: you.

Help me if you can. I would welcome a gentle reminder that you need
to be heard, need to express what's going on with you. And above all else,
please know that I really do care.

⊱◦◦⊰

Dear God, help us to be patient with one another when the distractions
of everyday life cause us to appear uncaring. Give each of us the courage to
nudge the other and deliver a gentle reminder of our commitment to each
other. Amen.

Wanna Go Out Tonight?

*David said to Abigail, "Blessed be the LORD, the God of Israel,
who sent you to meet me today!"*

1 SAMUEL 25:32 NRSV

My Dear Wife,

*I love being with you. Do you remember when I used to call and ask
you out? Then I'd come by your place and pick you up for a date? We'd be
all cleaned up and smelling good, and the anticipation was so thick I could
almost cut it with my pocketknife. Those were good days, and I don't see
any reason they can't keep on happening.*

*Let's go on an old-fashioned date again. Tell me how you'd like to do this
and where you'd like to go. Then let's just do it. I'll pull out all the stops:
wash the car, bring you flowers. I don't know about all the details, but let's
talk about it, make a plan, and carry it out—on a regular basis.*

---

*Dear God, help us to keep our love fresh and new—even if it seems to
take a little more work and planning. Show us ways to make a date special
for each other. Amen.*

Sometimes I Need Space

As those who have been chosen of God, holy and beloved, put on a heart of compassion, kindness, humility, gentleness and patience.

COLOSSIANS 3:12 NAS

My Dear Wife,

I appreciate your understanding heart. The workday occasionally seems to press in from all sides. Demands, decisions, deadlines. Somebody is always pushing for something. Sometimes when I get back home, I just want a little peace and quiet—and some space. I need to decompress and transform back into the man I want to be—someone I know you'll want to spend time with.

Be patient, my love, and give me a little space. I'll try to do the same for you, for I know your days can be trying, too, and I'm sure you appreciate this need for space just as much as I do.

Dear God, teach us to come to You in quietness and solitude, allowing You to refresh and restore our spirits. Help us to understand each other's need for a little time alone. Amen.

When I Come Home

Let us do our best to go into that place of rest, too, being careful not to disobey God ... thus failing to get in.

HEBREWS 4:11 TLB

My Dear Wife,

How you refresh my spirits. I look forward to coming home after a long day. Just to see our home—those little touches you've given that make it cozier and more comfortable—means so much to me. Most of all, I enjoy seeing your smiling face. It lights up my whole day. Everything else dims in comparison.

I know your days aren't always easy, and sometimes it's hard for you to simply paste on a smile. Let's try to understand each other in these moments and wait a bit before we bring out our expectations. But let's not waste too much time before we embrace and rejoice in our love, our marriage, our home.

Dear God, thank You for a happy and loving home that we both love coming home to. Give us patience and understanding as we come to each other at the end of a long day. Amen.

What Are Our Goals?

"I know what I am planning for you," says the Lord. "I have good plans for you, not plans to hurt you. I will give you hope and a good future."

JEREMIAH 29:11 NCV

My Dear Wife,

I love making plans with you. Goals are an important part of life and success, and I spend plenty of time pursuing them in my work. But sometimes I forget to pursue goals within our marriage, our family, and our home. Sometimes I get so caught up in other things that I just coast along, figuring our home life will somehow all fall neatly into place. Yet I know I need to lend a more active hand in this area and be a better leader.

I would welcome a chance to sit down with you and talk about our goals. I'd like to hear what you think, what you dream, and where you'd like to be, say, ten years from now. We need to include God in this, so let's also take time to ask Him to lead and direct us.

Dear God, please show us Your plan for our lives. We ask You to direct us and guide us to where You would have us go. Amen.

I Need Your Love

Let love be genuine . . . love one another with mutual affection;
outdo one another in showing honor.

ROMANS 12:9-10 NRSV

My Dear Wife,

Where would I be without you? You are as necessary to me as the air I breathe, the water that sustains me, the food that nourishes me, and God's love that cradles me. Yes, I need air, water, food, God's love—and I need your love, my dearest. I need your love just as surely as God blessed our union. How I thank God for leading me to you! Without you, I would be lost and hurting.

But that's how I feel, and I wanted you to know. I realize I don't always show you this vulnerable side of myself, and I'll admit it's a little uncomfortable. No guy likes to appear weak or needy, but I want you to understand how necessary you are to me. You play a vital role in my life. I need your love.

Dear God, it's a little bit scary needing someone's love so desperately. But then, that's how You made us, and we thank You. Amen.

When We Fight

"In your anger do not sin": Do not let the sun go down while you are still angry, and do not give the devil a foothold.

EPHESIANS 4:26-27 NIV

My Dear Wife,

I love it when we make up. I realize that disagreements are just a normal part of any marriage. And it's no secret that you and I don't always agree on everything. But it's my desire that we would never engage in hurtful words or accusations that are spoken in anger. Therefore, I make you these promises:

* I promise never to call you names.
* I promise not to dredge up old offenses.
* I promise to avoid phrases like "you always" and "you never."
* I promise to listen to what you are saying.
* I promise never to resort to physical aggression.
* I promise not to drag out an argument.
* I promise not to go to bed angry.

Dear God, teach us to live peaceably together, but if we need to clear the air, help us to do it in a healthy and wholesome way. And may our marriage be stronger for it. Amen

I Want to Listen Better

**My dear brothers and sisters,
always be willing to listen and slow to speak.**

JAMES 1:19 NCV

My Dear Wife,

I bless you for helping me listen. I want to improve my listening skills. I think I listen, really I do, but the truth is that I'm often too involved in my own thoughts to hear all you are saying.

I want to get better at listening, and I know that will only happen as I practice. It's like shooting hoops—I won't improve by sitting on the bench. I've got to get up off that bench and practice, over and over and over again, until I get it right. And just as I can improve my skills in any other endeavor, I can improve my listening skills with you. You make a good coach, sweetie, and I hope you'll keep on helping me in this area. Feel free to share your heart with me and tell me what you're thinking—it'll give me a good opportunity to learn to listen better.

Dear God, we're so glad You gave us two ears and one mouth. It helps us to appreciate how important it is for us to listen to each other. Amen.

Let's Light a Candle

My beloved said to me, "Rise up, my love, my fair one, and come away."

SONG OF SOLOMON 2:10 TLB

My Dear Wife,

Your love lights up my life. All right, I sometimes forget to be romantic. But right now, I want to make a plan to enjoy a peaceful evening with you, just the two of us. Let's play some romantic music. And let's light some of those scented candles you like so much. Because I'll admit it, my love, there is something very special about the warm glow of candlelight. I love the way it casts a rosy light across your pretty complexion.

Let's take lots of time to relax and simply enjoy the soft romantic light and atmosphere. We can talk quietly and with intimacy, just enjoying each other's presence. I love watching your eyes, luminescent and warm in the flickering candlelight.

Dear God, so often romance gets lost in the shuffle of our everyday lives. Remind us to do the little things that rekindle our love for each other. Amen.

How Can I Help You?

Each one must do just as he has purposed in his heart, not grudgingly or under compulsion, for God loves a cheerful giver.

2 CORINTHIANS 9:7 NAS

∽ⓔⓖ∾

My Dear Wife,

Thanks for encouraging me to help. It's not every day that I offer to help around the house, is it? Perhaps I'm afraid if I do, you'll hand me a long "honey-do" list and I'll end up spending a perfectly good Saturday cleaning gutters and fixing screens. Sometimes, though, I want you to give me the opportunity to offer my help before you ask.

I know that's not always easy. But perhaps there are some ways you can help get me on track. Sometimes just a gentle hint will do the trick. A good sense of humor will go a long way. I know you will find ways to draw me in, and I promise to respond with a good attitude. Truth is, it feels good to serve you and meet my family's needs.

∽ⓔⓖ∾

Dear God, help us to be sensitive to the things we can do to help each other and to carry through on them with a cheerful and positive attitude. Amen.

Healing Our Past

The LORD is close to the brokenhearted, and he saves those whose spirits have been crushed.

PSALM 34:18 NCV

My Dear Wife,

I bless you for sharing your heart with me. No one gets married without lugging along a little "extra baggage." Believe me, I'm aware that I, too, have brought along a few pieces of my own. And I know you have some as well. Maybe they are issues we're aware of, or perhaps we have things we'd forgotten or thought we'd left behind. But as we acknowledge them, understanding how old hurts from childhood and youth remain with us, we can begin to deal with them before they impact our relationship.

So, my goal is to share some of those old wounds, the ones that never quite seem to go away. And I hope you can tell me about your own. Because only then can we begin to understand one another. And perhaps we might even be able to pray for each other and support each other as we work together towards healing.

Dear God, show us how to be bring these old hurts to You, to pray for each other, and to look for Your healing touch. Amen.

Celebrating the Years

**Indeed, if a man should live many years,
let him rejoice in them all.**

ECCLESIASTES 11:8 NAS

⟳

My Dear Wife,

I bless you for the times we've shared. Sometimes the years go by so quickly that we hardly even notice. We become so caught up with all the demands of life and our grown-up responsibilities that we occasionally forget to pause and celebrate some of the milestones along the way. I certainly think that we have some achievements worth celebrating.

Let's remember to honor the time and energy we've invested in our relationship. Let's celebrate the fact that, through it all, we're still together—still in love and committed to our marriage and our lives together. Let's rejoice over our victories from the past, and let's look forward to our challenges in the future.

———⟳———

Dear God, we've been through so much together. Help us to remember our triumphs and celebrate our successes. And when we remember the hard times, help us to focus on Your goodness. Amen.

Come into My World

It is you, a person like me, my companion and good friend.

PSALM 55:13 NCV

ᕲᕉᕲ

My Dear Wife,

I love when our lives mesh. I know you think I live in my own little world sometimes, doing stuff like watching ball games, admiring a fine engine, or reading the latest sports magazine. But, hey, my world's not so bad. Once in a while, you should step in and see for yourself. Come on in and check it out.

I'd love to have your company when I visit a hardware store. I'd like it if you could share my enthusiasm for the gadgets that catch my fancy and incite my imagination. And I'd love to have your company when I attend a sporting event. It would double my fun to have you by my side rooting for our favorite team with me. And don't hesitate to invite me along with you occasionally, too. It's a good way for us to know each other better.

ᕲᕉᕲ

Dear God, show us new ways to share the different areas of our lives with each other. Amen.

When Disappointment Comes

Confess your trespasses to one another, and pray for one another that you may be healed.

JAMES 5:16 NKJV

My Dear Wife,

I'm sorry for letting you down. I know I don't always please you. And disappointment can take its toll on our relationship. Not only that, but I'm sure it affects how much you are able to trust me. And for that I am really sorry. I hope you can believe me, my love, when I say how much I hate to disappoint you. And I really do try to avoid doing so. Because when it happens, and it does, I am painfully aware of how it discourages you.

I will try not to make promises I can't keep, and I will work hard to keep my word to you, but I'm only human. I know I will let you down at times. When that happens, please remember that I love you and care about you more than words can say. And I hope you will give me a chance to make things right, if I can, and ask your forgiveness.

———

Dear God, teach us to be honorable in our promises to each other. Show us the importance of keeping our word. Amen.

Other People in Our Lives

For this reason a man shall leave his father and mother and be joined to his wife, and the two shall become one flesh.

MATTHEW 19:5 NAS

My Dear Wife,

I bless you for valuing me above others. Wouldn't it be great if it was just the two of us, all alone together—living in a little log cabin up in the mountains. Maybe then we might be perfectly happy. Well, at least for a while, until I wanted to go golfing, or until you needed to go shopping. But in real life, there's no way to avoid all those other people who come in and out of our lives, and it's no secret that they can seriously complicate things from time to time.

I know one thing I can do that should make it easier for you to deal with all those "others." I promise to place our relationship above all the rest. I believe that if you knew how much I love you, that it is more than I love my family, my work, even my best friend, then we could both relax and find peace no matter how many people are around us.

Dear God, help us to establish good priorities in our lives. Remind us to keep You in first place, our marriage in second, and others after that. Amen.

How You Can Help Me

**God opposes everyone who is proud,
but he is kind to everyone who is humble.**

JAMES 4:6 CEV

⸎

*M*y Dear Wife,

I love your touch on my life. I don't always act like I need you—it's just that I like to feel self-sufficient and capable. But, the fact is, there are all kinds of ways you can help me. And there are all kinds of times when I need your help. I sometimes give off an air of complete confidence, but the truth is that I need to know you back me, no matter what. And when I give up the bluff and invite you in, I'm always so glad I did.

It helps when I know you support what I do and who I am. I'm so glad that I have you, honey, and that you add your capabilities to mine and give us couple power. I like knowing that I can come home and find you ready to give whatever it is I seem to be needing. It may be a hug or a pep talk or a clean dressing for my wounds. And it helps when you just plain love me—sweet and simple.

⸎

*D*ear God, *thanks for making us partners for life. Teach us to avail ourselves to that gracious gift you have given us. Amen.*

There Are Things I Don't Understand

**By wisdom a house is built,
and through understanding it is established.**

PROVERBS 24:3 NIV

My Dear Wife,

I bless you for explaining. I don't like to come across as dense, but sometimes it seems there's just so much I don't understand about you. Sometimes it seems that we just look at things from a different angle, and I need your help when I can't quite see something in the same way as you do. I guess every couple experiences those times when they don't seem to be on the same page.

I promise to be sensitive to your needs, but I know I'll miss it at times. Let me know when that happens. Just tell me: "Hey you, I need a hug . . . I need some space . . . I need a cup of hot tea." Just let me know, okay? I love you and I want to you to know that I care.

Dear God, there will be times when we just aren't in sync. When those times come, help us to speak up courageously and kindly. Amen.

I Want to Listen

Love one another with mutual affection;
outdo one another in showing honor.

ROMANS 12:10 NRSV

My Dear Wife,

I really do need your gentle nudges. Without a doubt, I know I can appear to be totally absorbed in my own world. I can get caught up in my career, or some project I want to finish around the house, or even my own hobbies. And it probably seems like I'm shutting you out. And maybe I am, but I don't mean to. I guess I just feel a sense of responsibility to do my best for you and our family. But just the same, I don't want to be so consumed that I can't pause and take time for you. Because you're worth it, my love.

So when I'm buried in some project, and I forget that you need to be heard. Go ahead and nudge me, remind me that you're waiting—that you need a moment of my time. Because you are important to me! And I really want to be there for you.

Dear God, remind us that we're committed to be available to one another. Nudge us when it's time to listen to You and to each other. Amen.

An Evening with You

Take me away with you—let us hurry!

SONG OF SOLOMON 1:4 NIV

My Dear Wife,

I love it when we're together. Shall we dine at a fancy restaurant, go to the theatre, or enjoy a moonlit cruise across the bay? Or perhaps a romantic evening together doesn't need to break the bank, take days of preparation, or require a tux. Maybe it would be better, not to mention more romantic, to do something simple.

To be honest, all I really want is a quiet evening with you. The two of us all alone—it might even be better if we stay home. Maybe I can help you fix a simple meal. Or maybe we can take a stroll around the block. Or how about a game of chess? But whatever we decide upon, let's do it together—just you and me and romance.

Dear God, remind us to plan some special, quiet moments—intimate times for just the two of us. And help us to remember that the important thing is simply being together. Amen.

Seize the Day!

This is the day that the LORD has made;
let us rejoice and be glad in it.

PSALM 118:24 NIV

❦

*M*y Dear Wife,

I love your spontaneity. I admit I can become too focused on the minor details of life—things that aren't terribly significant. And as a result, I sometimes almost forget to enjoy some of the most important moments of living. Occasionally I need you to remind me to cease from my activity for long enough to really seize the day.

I forget that only God knows how many of these earthly days we'll have to enjoy together. How many moments will I relish you in my arms or hear your sweet words of love and affection whispered in my ear? And when it's all said and done, I won't regret using my time for such pleasures. I hope you will remind me to enjoy what we have together—to welcome each new day as a living gift from God.

❦

*D*ear God, only You know the span of our lives—but whether they're short or long, each day is unique and special and worthy of celebration. Teach us to pause and welcome them. Amen.

Let's Take a Walk

**The leaves are coming out and the grape vines are in blossom.
How delicious they smell! Arise, my love, my fair one,
and come away.**

SONG OF SOLOMON 2:13 TLB

‿◉◠

My Dear Wife,

I love aligning my pace to yours. How invigorating and romantic it is to take a walk with the one you love! Maybe it's the warm feeling of your hand in mine. Or the comfortable sense of moving along without rushing. Or perhaps it's the changing season, or the look of the landscape, or simply the rhythmic sound of footsteps falling into pace—almost like a dance.

Will you come walk with me, my love? Can we breathe the fresh air and enjoy some exercise, along with the rejuvenation of our spirits and souls? And let's talk as we go; I want to hear about your day. Or maybe we'll just enjoy the quiet around us—the sounds of birds or the gentle breeze whispering through the treetops.

‿◉◠

Dear God, simple pleasures can be incredibly romantic. Remind us that they are often just a footstep away. Amen.

A Five-Minute Exercise

**Before the dawn comes and the shadows flee away,
come back to me, my love.**

SONG OF SOLOMON 2:17 NLT

My Dear Wife,

I love the touch of your hands. Now I know this might sound a little corny, and I'm usually not one to indulge in such things. But please hear me out. You see, I think we can become so comfortable around each other that we forget to notice certain things—or maybe we start taking each other for granted. So some night, when it's quiet and calm, let's do this little exercise together.

Let's sit on the floor, cross-legged, if we can, and face each other. Then let's reach out and touch our palms together, just lightly. Without speaking, let's just look into each other's faces—I promise not to giggle—and enjoy the sensation of touching palms. Then let's close our eyes and "read" each other's faces with our fingertips.

Dear God, sometimes, funny little things like this can open wonderful new doors in a relationship, helping us to see each other in fresh new ways. Give us the courage to try. Amen.

Stand by Your Man

I will sing of your strength,
in the morning I will sing of your love;
for you are my fortress,
my refuge in times of trouble.

PSALM 59:16 NIV

*M*y Dear Wife,

I love knowing you're backing me. Occasionally I want a fresh challenge. I want to take on something new or stretch my ordinary world in some different way. At other times, it may seem daunting to step out of my norm and take a chance. And, to be honest, I'm not always as confident as I try to appear. If the risk seems too big, I might not even step up to the plate.

These are the times when I most appreciate your support. To know you're standing behind me, backing me, and cheering me on makes a huge difference. You may have no idea how much your encouragement means to me. Not only that, it makes me feel so connected to you—like we're in this together-and our success is shared!

---

*D*ear God, thank You for the encouragement You bring to our lives and the support of our friends and family. Most of all, thank You for the support of a faithful spouse. Amen.

Just Tell Me You Love Me

Show me your face,
let me hear your voice;
for your voice is sweet,
and your face is lovely.

SONG OF SOLOMON 2:14 NIV

My Dear Wife,

I love to hear you say it. Of course, I should know that you love me. And you show me your love by all the little things you do, day after day. And certainly, I've heard those three little words, so many times before. But even so, they are so important to me!

Do you know how much I need to hear those three little words? I need you to whisper them in my ear at night. And I need to see your eyes in the morning light as you say them aloud. Somehow this convinces me that you really mean it. Oh, I know it's not only the words, but this is the stuff our relationship is made of. And I won't get tired of hearing you say it. So, go ahead, sweetheart, say it again.

Dear God, thank You for pouring Your love into our hearts so that we would know the true meaning of love. Remind us often that we need to speak and hear our words of love. Amen.

Let's Make a Plan

The LORD will guide you always;
he will satisfy your needs in a sun-scorched land
and will strengthen your frame.
You will be like a well-watered garden,
like a spring whose waters never fail.

ISAIAH 58:11 NIV

My Dear Wife,

I love how your mind works. How about if we sit down together and make some sort of plan? Maybe it could be for a family vacation or just a weekend together. Or how about a home-improvement project? Whatever we decide, I think it would be fun to do it together. I like hearing your ideas, and it's good for us to cooperate with each other. I know I might try your patience from time to time, but I'd like to learn how to give and take—not to mention how it might help improve my ability to listen to you.

Then we finally complete whatever it is that we decide to do, we can enjoy the rewards of our labor. For we'll have learned to work as a team to accomplish something. And, together, we can celebrate our victory!

Dear God, help us to find a plan we can carry out together. We know it won't all go smoothly, but it'll be well worth the effort. In the end, we'll be closer than when we started. Amen.

What's Really Important

**And he answering said, Thou shalt love the Lord thy God with
all thy heart, and with all thy soul, and with all thy strength,
and with all thy mind; and thy neighbour as thyself.**

LUKE 10:27 KJV

My Dear Wife,

You matter to me. We both experience daily tugs and pulls on our lives,
demanding our time and attention. Often I find the most urgent things
pretend to be the most important. And sometimes I mistakenly give those
pressing issues my top priority. But if I can just step back and get a better
perspective, I sometimes figure out that those urgent things aren't all that
vital.

When I take time to consider things, I usually remember what's most
important in life. Thankfully, it's pretty simple—almost embarrassingly so.
And so, because I love you, my dear, I want to remind you, as well. First
of all, I know it's crucial that we love God with our whole hearts. Next,
it's essential to love each other. Then everyone and everything else simply
comes after that.

Dear God, help us to keep our priorities straight and simple. Don't
allow us to get caught up in the tyranny of the urgent. Amen.

Your Deepest Hurt

For You have delivered my soul from death,
My eyes from tears,
And my feet from falling.

PSALM 116:8 NKJV

My Dear Wife,

I bless you for trusting me with your pain. Perhaps there are things about you, your past life, that you've yet to tell me—or perhaps you've mentioned, but we never really talked about it. And it's possible you may need to tell me again. For it seems certain that we both have some old hurts in our lives—perhaps some we've even inflicted on each other. But how will our deepest hurts ever heal if we leave them hidden and buried? And even if they can't heal overnight, surely we can start the healing process now.

Do you need to tell me about a past hurt, my love? If so, I am here for you. I want to hear all you have to say. And then I hope we can pray about it. Can we ask God to continue the healing work that He's begun in both of us? Together, let's believe that He can make us whole.

Dear God, help us to be there for each other when it's convenient and when it hurts. Give us a heart to listen and a heart to pray. Amen.

My Dreams

Every day and all night long their counsel will lead you and save you from harm; when you wake up in the morning, let their instructions guide you into the new day.

PROVERBS 6:22 TLB

∽⊙⌒∾

My Dear Wife,

I bless you for listening to my dreams. I have some dreams tucked safely in my heart—some desires, some longings, some hopes, and aspirations. But sometimes I try to push them down, suppress them, keeping them out of sight and out of mind. It can be unsettling to dream because it often upsets the status quo and rocks the boat.

But then it will occur to me, aren't dreams what life, at least a good and fulfilling life, is made of? And if we quit dreaming, don't we in essence cease to live? So perhaps it's better to welcome our dreams, whether they're big or small, and bring them out into the light of day, discussing them openly. We might even find that our dreams are the same.

∽⊙⌒∾

Dear God, You are the One who gives us our dreams, implanting them in the recesses of our hearts. Show us how to open our hearts to each other and follow the path You have placed before us. Amen.

You're My Sweetness

How much better than wine is your love,
And the scent of your perfumes
Than all spices!

SONG OF SOLOMON 4:10 NKJV

My Dear Wife,

I bless you for the pleasures you bring me. Do you know how much I enjoy every little thing about you? The smell of your hair, the softness of your skin, the way you smile at my jokes? Do you know how I love the feel of your hands, the shape of your neck, that fragrance you wear? You are the sweetness in my life, dear one. You are my sugar and spice and everything nice.

And without your sweet touch, my life would be like a cake made without adding sugar. It would be like a garden without any flowers or a rainbow in black and white. For you are my sweetness, my music, my color, and my warmth. You make my world a richer, finer, better place. And I thank God for sharing you with me.

Dear God, thank You for the little things that sweeten and brighten our lives. Amen.

Around the House

Through knowledge its rooms are filled with rare and beautiful treasures.

PROVERBS 24:4 NIV

My Dear Wife,

I bless you for your touch in our home. Sometimes I might act like I don't care too much about how our home looks. And maybe I do that because it feels more like your territory and I don't want to invade your space. Or maybe it's just because I'm not sure how to get more involved.

When I look around me, I enjoy the subtle but tangible expression of your personality. But I want to start viewing our home differently. I want to see it as an extension of the two of us—a melding together of our personalities, a place where we can both feel comfortable. I also want our home to be a place we can share with others. And I can see how this shouldn't all fall onto your shoulders. So, tell me how I can help.

Dear God, teach us to work together in our home. Show us ways we can make our home into a place of peace and order and beauty-a place where people will walk in and sense Your presence. Amen.

Over the Years

I will be your God throughout your lifetime—until your hair is white with age. I made you, and I will care for you. I will carry you along and save you.

ISAIAH 46:4 NLT

∞⊙∞

*M*y Dear Wife,

I bless you for caring for our marriage. Building our marriage reminds me of building a house. If we take the time and invest the energy, it should protect and sustain us throughout the oncoming years. And when I consider the future, I smile as I imagine us growing older together, getting closer, our relationship deepening with time. For I think a love like ours can only improve with age.

Like a sturdy, well-built, older home, with mature landscaping and a handsome patina to the woodwork, I imagine our marriage growing more and more attractive with each passing year. But like an older home, I know we'll have to keep it up with careful maintenance—for neglect can lead to ruin. Our reward will be a warm, cozy haven of love.

∞⊙∞

*D*ear God, teach us to recognize the everyday increasing value of our marriage. Show us how to care for it as if it were a priceless investment—which, in fact, it is. Amen.

Mixed Memories

**It is good and pleasant when God's people
live together in peace!**

PSALM 133:1 NCV

⌒⊙⌒

My Dear Wife,

I love how you remember things. Do you remember every detail of the first time we met? I think it's printed indelibly in my mind, and yet, if we compared notes, I bet we would remember things quite differently. Why is that?

I'm sure it's just because we see things differently—I view life through my eyes and my experience, and you see it through yours. Neither of us are completely right or wrong. We just have a different perspective. Consider two people describing the same house, one from inside and one from the outside. One declares the house is blue and the other says the house is white—and although they can't agree on the color, they're both exactly right.

⌒⊙⌒

Dear God, help us not only to respect our different perspectives, but also to enjoy the varied interest we both bring to this marriage. We thank You once again for our uniqueness. Amen.

Holidays Throw Me for a Loop

Forget the former things; do not dwell on the past. See, I am doing a new thing!

ISAIAH 43:18-19 NIV

My Dear Wife,

I bless you for caring about holidays. There's no escaping that holidays and birthdays and various celebrations come at us like clockwork—and they never seem to stop. But I think I'm coming to realize that due to our unique backgrounds and upbringing, we perceive these special occasions differently. For we both bring a unique set of expectations and customs into our marriage. And I admit that I sometimes forget how we were both raised differently.

These individual expectations can cause us to be disappointed or frustrated because important days don't go just the way we'd hoped. And I admit, it's often my fault. Let's discuss these special times in advance and see if we can build new traditions of our own.

Dear God, show us how to create new traditions for our family, borrowing from the special things we have each brought into our marriage. Amen.

Sometimes I Watch You

How beautiful you are, my darling,
How beautiful you are!

SONG OF SOLOMON 4:1 NAS

✦

My Dear Wife,

How I love to see you. Sometimes, when I know you're not looking, I watch you. Perhaps you're interacting with a girlfriend, intently focusing on something in the kitchen, or just rousing from sleep. I like to study your face—the curve of your nose, the shape of your earlobe, the way your hair frames your face.

But even more than that, I like to watch your facial expressions. The way your brow slightly creases with concern when you see someone you love facing a tough situation. I like the way you grow thoughtful when someone asks a provoking question. Or how your lip just barely twitches when you're trying not to laugh.

✦

Dear God, You have given us so many little things to love and enjoy about each other. Help us never to take those familiar expressions or unique qualities for granted. Amen.

When I'm Tired . . .

Worry weighs a person down;
an encouraging word cheers a person up.

PROVERBS 12:25 NLT

*M*y Dear Wife,

I love how you refresh me. I wish it weren't so, but sometimes the
everyday stresses take a lot out of me. And when I come home I'm tired
and fatigued. Like an engine running on empty, I start to slow down and
lag behind. A lot of the time, I don't even notice how or when it happened.

It's times like these when I really need you. I need your patience and
your understanding and your gentle encouragement. Perhaps I even need
you to remind me that it's time to slow down, that I need to take it easy.
Or maybe you can point out how I've neglected to get sufficient rest in my
frenzy-paced world. Because the truth is, I often do focus too much on
work and getting things done—and a loving reminder from you can
prevent me from getting weary.

*D*ear God, help us both to find balance in our daily lives and to
remind each other to include enough time for rest and fun. Amen.

You Are So Beautiful

Your beauty should come from within you—the beauty of a gentle and quiet spirit that will never be destroyed and is very precious to God.

1 PETER 3:4 NCV

My Dear Wife,

I bless you for your many layers of beauty. I know I don't tell you nearly enough, and I suppose it could seem that I take it for granted—but you are beautiful to me. And not just on the surface, either. Your beauty begins deep from within your heart and spirit—and from there it flows throughout your entire being—from head to toe.

I know you don't see yourself the way I do. You can be critical of your looks, and you tend to focus on what you perceive as flaws. But take my word, darling, you are beautiful to me. Look at your eyes through my eyes. I don't think I'll ever tire of looking at you. Even as we both age, I know your beauty will remain, emanating from your spirit and flowing throughout your life.

Dear God, help us to see each other through the eyes of love and to appreciate the beauty resident in each of us. Amen.

You Make Me Complete

The Lord God said, "It isn't good for man to be alone; I will make a companion for him, a helper suited to his needs."

GENESIS 2:18 TLB

My Dear Wife,

I love how you make me whole. I always thought of myself as a complete person, fairly self-sufficient and capable. That was before I met you. Now I feel like something was missing. Because I believe being married to you has somehow made me more complete. I don't even understand, nor can I explain exactly how this little miracle works. But I think it's just another one of God's wonderful mysteries. And I'm immensely thankful for it.

You help me to grow on a daily basis—in ways that nothing else can. And because of you, I honestly believe I am becoming a "bigger" and better person. Your kindness and gentleness has taught me to love and forgiveness. And I hope there are things you can learn from me.

Dear God, we are grateful that You have given us to each other. Help us always to appreciate the balance and completion we each bring to the other's life. Amen.

The Way We Were

I remember the days of old;
I meditate on all Your doings;
I muse on the work of Your hands.

PSALM 143:5 NAS

My Dear Wife,

I love to remember how far we've come. I enjoy looking at photos from the early years in our relationship. We've sure changed, and I don't just mean our physical appearance. We've changed in deeper ways too. When I pause to remember where we've been, I really begin to appreciate how far we've come together. And I know our love has grown over the years. But I must also ask myself: Have we left anything valuable behind?

Do you recall how we were back then? Maybe we were overly idealistic, and perhaps somewhat unrealistic. But did we dream big dreams back then? Have we forgotten some? And how did we see the world in which we live? Were we simplistic? Overwhelmed? Hopeful? I want to remember the way we were—and ask ourselves how and why we've become who we are.

Dear God, thank You for reminding us that understanding the past can help us better appreciate the present and plan for the future. Amen.

Let's Turn Down the Lights

You have made my heart beat faster with a single glance of your eyes.

SONG OF SOLOMON 4:9 NAS

My Dear Wife,

You are the spark that ignites my heart. What is it about turning the lights down low? It's as if something amazing happens. You add a little candlelight, combined with some nice soft music, and it's a formula for romance. I love to see how an intimate feeling settles over a dimly lit room, and how the playful shadows seem to push away the distractions of life.

And the world falls away, and it's just you and me, my love, alone at last in our undisturbed and private world. You are my focus, and I hope I am yours. For now, we can sit together, enjoy quiet conversation, sweet nuances, the pleasure of familiarity, the expectation of things to come. So, may I turn down the lights, my love?

Dear God, thank You for the gift of intimacy. As we spend time, just the two of us, getting to know each other better, help us to find a new level of commitment to one another. Amen.

I'm Here for You

Though one might prevail against another,
two will withstand one.
A threefold cord is not quickly broken.

ECCLESIASTES 4:12 NRSV

My Dear Wife,

I love when you need me. I love the way you always support me, encouraging me in my job, standing behind me through difficulties. And I sometimes feel guilty that I'm not always that supportive of you. But I want to be. And I want to get better at showing it. Because I do believe in you. I think you're smart and talented and capable.

I want you to know that I'm here for you. I'm standing behind and beside you. And I hope and believe the very best for you and your life. Your success is my success. And by the same token, I will share in your disappointments. So whatever comes, my love, for better or worse, I will stand by you.

Dear God, teach us to be faithful to support each other, following Your example of commitment and love. Amen.

Sometimes I'm Distracted

**Accept my teachings and learn from me,
because I am gentle and humble in spirit,
and you will find rest for your lives.**

MATTHEW 11:29 NCV

⋘◉◎⋙

*M*y Dear Wife,

I bless you for knowing when to slow down. You know how I can get so focused on accomplishing something, and getting a certain job done, that I almost lose sight of what's going on around me. I know how we guys often tend to set our sights too tightly in one area, shoving anything we perceive as distractions aside. But I'm sorry for when I've treated you like that. Because you are not a distraction. You are the best part of my life.

But I invite your help, during those stressful times. Go ahead and gently remind me to slow down and to keep my priorities straight. And if you feel neglected, please let me know, and then let's work together to slow things down.

⋘◉◎⋙

*D*ear God, it's easy to get too busy and let our priorities slip. Remind us to keep our lives in balance. Amen.

Please Forgive Me

Bear with each other and forgive whatever grievances you may have against one another. Forgive as the Lord forgave you.

COLOSSIANS 3:13 NIV

My Dear Wife,

I thank you for your gracious spirit. No one likes to admit it—especially me—but it's true, I actually do blow it from time to time. And I'm sure there have been plenty of times when I didn't say I was sorry—not to mention the times when I never even paused to ask you to forgive me. Oh, I could try to make excuses now, but they would probably just boil down to things like selfishness or pride—so I won't bother.

Instead, I want to say I'm truly sorry for all the times I've hurt you and haven't apologized. And I'm sorry that I didn't always ask you to forgive me. But I thank you for the times you forgave me anyway. Your forgiveness means more to me than I can even say. It's like a stream of fresh-flowing water, quenching a thirsty soul.

Dear God, You have always impressed on us the importance of forgiveness. Help us to be quick and unswerving in our commitment to forgive completely, burying no offense. Amen.

When I Think of You

*Build yourselves up in your most holy faith
and pray in the Holy Spirit.*

JUDE 20 NIV

My Dear Wife,

Thoughts of you are a comfort to me. When I'm in the midst of a trying situation or I'm wont to understand why the whole world has turned against me, you come to mind. And just the thought of you brings me encouragement and comfort. Maybe it's because I can imagine your loving, tender embrace, your sweet smile, or the comforting words of love and kindness you whisper in my ear.

Somehow just thinking of you brings a sense of stability and peace to my world. And I become so grateful for you, looking forward to when we come back together at the day's end. I look forward to how you'll listen to my battle tales and console me with your good humor!

Dear God, we thank You for our relationship, for the joy and the comfort it brings to both of us. Thank You also for our relationship with You, without which none of our other relationships would be possible or profitable. Amen.

I Need Your Affection

When I found him whom my soul loves;
I held on to him and would not let him go.

SONG OF SOLOMON 3:4 NAS

My Dear Wife,

I bless you for reaching out to me. Whether I admit it or not, I have all kinds of needs. And most of those needs are met by you—from a clean pair of matching socks to a freshly pressed pair of slacks to a delicious homemade meal. And then sometimes I simply need you to nestle in my arms, run your fingers through my hair, or tell me everything's going to work out just fine. And it will, with you beside me.

I might not always admit how much I need your affection. Maybe there's something inside us that doesn't like to acknowledge such deeply felt needs. Maybe we're afraid of what would happen if those needs were denied. But the fact is I do need your loving touch—your affection. For your touch reminds me of your love.

Dear God, teach us to swallow foolish pride and reach out to each other for the things that we both need. Amen.

Accepting My Friends

**Do not forsake your own friend
or your father's friend.**

PROVERBS 27:10 NKJV

⌒⌒

My Dear Wife,

I appreciate your kindness to my friends. All right, I'll admit it——my friends aren't always what you consider perfect gentlemen. Some of my buddies are rather rough around the edges, and even I wonder about them at times! But they've stuck by me in some hard situations, and they're like brothers to me. By the same token, I don't always appreciate your friends either. But just as you and I are different (and we're learning to accept and appreciate those differences), our friends are different, too.

I know you don't always enjoy being around my friends, but I appreciate the fact that you are kind and generous to them for my sake. It makes me feel very good to realize that you try to see good things in them simply because I do. It means a lot.

⌒⌒

Dear God, You are the best of all friends. Give us the grace to love and respect the people we each call friends. Amen.

My Best Friend

There are "friends" who pretend to be friends, but there is a friend who sticks closer than a brother.

PROVERBS 18:24 TLB

M*y Dear Wife,*

I thank you for your loyal friendship. I think the best marriages begin with strong friendships. It's like the foundation that steadily holds the whole relationship together. I've watched couples who have learned to appreciate similar things, but more than that they seem to appreciate each other's company. And those seem like the marriages built to travel the distance. And that's what I want for us. I want to be your best friend, my love, and I want you to be mine.

I realize it takes time and commitment to become best friends, but I'm sure it's worth it. I want us to depend on each other. So, let's set our friendship above all others. Let's commit to spend both quantity and quality time together. Let's pursue common interests, and let's watch our friendship grow.

D*ear God, help us build a lasting friendship. Teach us about commitment and love. Show us ways to develop similar interests. Join our hearts as friends. Amen.*

Fanning the Flame

How fair and how pleasant you are,
O love, with your delights!

Song of Solomon 7:6 NKJV

❧◦❧

My Dear Wife,

I love those simple things you do. Occasionally it can feel as if the embers of romance are burning low in me. Maybe I'm tired or I've had a particularly hard week. Sometimes, I'm concerned about finances or a heavy workload. I try not to let the mundane interfere with our relationship, but most of the time I'm not too successful at blotting out the things that press on my mind. That's when you really shine, my love.

You always remember the simple little things that warm my heart—things like a gentle shoulder massage or a certain look. My favorite dessert or a soft tender caress. And sometimes it's just knowing how much you love me, how important I am to you, how you respect me for who I am, and that you'll stand by me unconditionally, that makes all the difference.

❧◦❧

Dear God, thank You for providing comfort and solace through the blessings of marriage. Help us to always remember the importance of the simple things. Amen.

You Are Quite a Woman!

It is hard to find a good wife,
because she is worth more than rubies.
Her husband trusts her completely.
With her, he has everything he needs.

PROVERBS 31:10-11 NCV

My Dear Wife,

I bless you for your many gifts. Have I told you lately how impressed I am by you? Have I mentioned how much I admire all you are or how much I respect all that you do? You're really quite a woman, and I'm thankful God gave you to me. And I know being a woman isn't all that easy these days. I know that it's a juggling act to keep all your responsibilities in order.

I want to learn to be more helpful and supportive with all the things you're trying to accomplish. But I need your help. I need you to tell me how I can lighten your load or brighten your day. Because I know that although you're quite a woman, you're not a superwoman. And I'm sure relieved—for you know I'm not a superman.

Dear God, thank You for giving us to each other and initiating the love that flows between us. Show us ways to help each other more. Help us to communicate when we're in need. Amen.

Let's Take Some Time

**There is an appointed time for everything.
And there is a time for every event under heaven.**

ECCLESIASTES 3:1 NAS

᳁

My Dear Wife,

I love to be with you. Too many times we say we'll do something special, or we'll go do that when we have the time. But how quickly time can slip away before we actually keep these promises. So, right now, instead of waiting until we have the time—I want us to decide that we will take the time, and then let's not put it off.

So how about if we both sit down with our calendars and make a specific plan together. We can block out some time that belongs only to us—to our relationship, to our marriage. Whether it's a few days away, or a weekly date night, or meeting downtown for lunch—let's get it in writing and commit to do it. We are worth taking the time for.

Dear God, only You know how many days we have to spend together in this life. Help us find the time we need for our relationship and give us the tenacity to make it happen. Amen.

Totally Devoted

Greater love has no one than this, that one lay down his life for his friends.

JOHN 15:13 NAS

My Dear Wife,

I am devoted to you. How can anyone ever forget the romantic story of Romeo and Juliet? Those two loved each other so totally that they were willing to die for each other. Sure, they were both teenagers, not to mention fictional—but just the same, I'd like to be that devoted to you!

I know these words are easier said than done, and I'll probably never get the chance to actually lay down my life for you physically, but I know I can do it emotionally—probably on a daily basis. I want to improve at placing you and your needs above my own. I can get better at dying to my own selfishness and pride. I know it won't be easy, but I want to show my devotion to you.

Dear God, perhaps that sort of selfless, loving devotion can come only from You. Teach us to love each other so fully that we would gladly lay down our own areas of selfishness for the other. Amen.

Something You Don't Know . . .

Can you fathom the mysteries of God?
Can you probe the limits of the Almighty?
They are higher than the heavens—what can you do?
They are deeper than the depths of the grave—
what can you know?

JOB 11:7-8 NIV

My Dear Wife,

We have places to explore. Without a doubt, you know me very well—probably better than anyone on earth. But, I wonder if you are aware that there are still some hidden places in my heart. Places where you have not yet been. Places I long to share with you.

These are things that require time and trust. And they cannot be rushed. But I'm sure that over time, I will one by one open them up to you. And when those times come, we can explore, hand in hand, these hidden parts of my innermost self, together.

Dear God, so often we hesitate to reveal ourselves to each other and to You. What we forget is that You know us better than we know ourselves. Amen.

Let's Dance

You will . . . be happy and dance merrily with timbrels.

JEREMIAH 31:4 TLB

❧◉❧

My Dear Wife,

I love how you feel in my arms. How about if we listen to some great music—something we both like a lot—something that makes us want to tap our toes and even get onto our feet and move to the rhythm? It can be fast and energetic, or it can be slow and soulful. But let's just let the music flow right through us, and then let's toss our inhibitions aside and really dance.

I love being close to you as we enjoy the music and the moment and the fun. And our souls seem to meld together as our feet move us across the floor. How long has it been since we've dipped and twirled and glided across our candlelit patio to the sounds of the Beetles or Benny Goodman or Barbra Streisand? So, come on, baby, let's dance.

❧◉❧

Dear God, help us as we look for ways to relax and have fun together, whether it's listening to classical music together or doing our own version of the rumba. Amen.

Total Honesty

Speaking the truth in love, we will in all things grow up into him who is the Head, that is, Christ.

EPHESIANS 4:15 NIV

My Dear Wife,

I bless you for speaking in love. It hardly needs to be said that any healthy relationship needs a solid foundation of honesty and openness beneath it. And I want for us to have that too. So, I hope you'll always feel you can be totally candid with me, even if it's not always totally comfortable. Let's not back away from anything that bothers us. For how will we ever grow and develop in our relationship if we sidestep the truth? And isn't it truth that will ultimately free us?

I promise you I will always remember that love must accompany truth—truth without love can be hurtful and destructive. And when you need to be honest with me, I agree to listen even if it hurts a little.

Dear God, we need honesty in our relationship. Show us how to speak the truth in love. Teach us to respond with wisdom and dignity, and help us to grow closer together. Amen.

When We Pray Together

All things for which you pray and ask, believe that you have received them, and they will be granted you.

MARK 11:24 NAS

My Dear Wife,

I need you as my spiritual partner. I'll admit, it's not always the easiest thing to do. And I can usually think of many excuses why we shouldn't— like it's too late or too early, or we're too busy or too tired. I don't know why, but it usually seems easier to not pray together. And yet it's incredible when we do actually sit down and pray together, because something amazing often happens inside of me. I feel as if our hearts and souls become united somehow—as if, by God's power, we become spiritually connected.

But even so, it can be difficult for me to invite you to pray. For some reason I just put it off. Perhaps we need a regular time. Maybe I need a gentle reminder from you. Let's find some ways to ensure that we regularly join our hearts in prayer.

Dear God, help us come together to decide how we can become better prayer partners. Amen.

I'm Lost without You

Two are better than one. . . . If two lie down together they keep warm, but how can one be warm alone?

ECCLESIASTES 4:9,11 NAS

❧

$\mathcal{M}$y Dear Wife,

You are such a vital part of me. I know you think I'm a fairly independent person—able to move with confidence as I conquer my way through life. And I can act as if I need little if any help from others. But the truth is, if you're away from me, even for just a day or two, I start feeling pretty lost without you. It's a somewhat unsettling feeling. But in some ways, it's a relief, too.

It's when I'm missing you that I realize how interconnected we really are. Like a good wake-up call, I realize how vital you are to me and how empty my life would be without you. For I need you, my love. I want you sleeping right next to me. I need your sweet smile to start my day. I need your hand in mine. For with you, I am found.

❧

$\mathcal{D}$ear God, thank You for the comfort and strength we receive when we fully understand that we belong to each other and to You. Amen.

How Do I Love Thee?

Her children rise up and call her blessed;
Her husband also, and he praises her:
"Many daughters have done well,
But you excel them all."

PROVERBS 31:28-29 NKJV

My Dear Wife,

I bless you for all that you are. Some people might count their blessings as they go to sleep. But sometimes I think I might like to count how many things I love about you—that's a blessing in itself. For starters, I love the touch of your fingers on my skin and the pretty twinkle in your eye when we share a private joke. I love how you call me up at work sometimes just because you want to hear the sound of my voice.

I love to wrap my arm around your waist. I love the soft feel of your hand in mine as we walk. I love the shape of your lips as they curve into a sweet smile. I love the way you cry at a movie when you think no one's watching. I love you!

Dear God, we ask You to help make our love grow like a well-watered garden in springtime. We ask that You'll show us new ways to share and communicate our love for each other. Amen.

When We Are Old

**White hair is a crown of glory
and is seen most among the godly.**

PROVERBS 16:31 TLB

My Dear Wife,

Our love grows better with time. Do you ever imagine the two us years from now? Will you have snowy white hair? Will I grow bald? With fading eyes and wrinkling skin, will our frames bend with the passing of time? Do you ever wonder if our love can remain as fresh and alive as that day we repeated our wedding vows? I sure hope so. But it mystifies me how something as seemingly fragile as love can survive the effects of time and age—how it can endure the everyday hurts of living.

I sometimes catch my reflection—the aging process in motion—and I wonder, will you still love me when my muscles sag, when my strength is gone? I believe that you will, and I promise that age will not diminish my love for you.

Dear God, as human beings we often struggle with insecurities. Remind us often that our love is anchored securely in our hearts. And as we give ourselves daily to You and to each other, our relationship will grow stronger with age. Amen.

Simple Things

*So continuing daily with one accord . . . breaking bread from
house to house, they ate their food
with gladness and simplicity of heart.*

ACTS 2:46 NKJV

⌒⌒⌒

My Dear Wife,

*Thanks for all the simple pleasures. I'm sure you know by now that I'm
a fairly simple creature. The things that make me happy aren't too difficult
to come by. I enjoy things like good food—there's nothing quite like a
delicious, home-cooked meal. Another thing I enjoy is the peaceful quiet
when we're alone just before we retire for the night. And, darling, I so
value the respect and love you give me.*

*But too often I catch myself grasping for things that complicate and
confuse our lives. I'm so sorry when that happens. Please be patient with
me and don't hesitate to remind me that I feel the most happiness and peace
when I am appreciating the simple things.*

⌒⌒⌒

*Dear God, help us each to always put the other first and remind us
when we become selfish and self-centered. Amen.*

God's Touch on Our Lives

*God began doing a good work in you, and I am sure he will
continue it until it is finished.*

PHILIPPIANS 1:6 NCV

My Dear Wife,

*I love how God is changing us. Something happens on a regular basis, as
we move through our days, responding to life's challenges, trying to do
what's right, working to get ahead—God places His touch on our lives. In
those moments, He quietly administers His grace, protection, mercy, and
love into our everyday routines. I know it happens a lot. And I wonder
how many times I've neglected to even pause and take notice.*

*I can see God's touch on our marriage, too, my love. Looking back I can
see how He's preserved and watched over us, how He binds our hearts
together, how He strengthens our love. He even teaches us to forgive each
other. I want to take time to acknowledge Him.*

*Dear God, we thank You and praise You for Your faithful touch on our
lives. Help us not to take Your touch for granted. We know that our
relationship and marriage is a gift from You. Amen.*

Giving Gifts

You are generous because of your faith. And I am praying that you will really put your generosity to work, for in so doing you will come to an understanding of all the good things we can do for Christ.

PHILEMON 1:6 NLT

My Dear Wife,

I love your generous heart. It's great to give someone a gift. And I love it when I can surprise you with something special. Because I really do enjoy the act of being generous—it seems to strengthen and invigorate my heart. And I know that those of us, fortunate enough to be on the giving end, really do get the best part of the blessing—for I'm sure that it's more fun to give a gift than to receive one.

But could it be that the act of giving might be even more fulfilling if we did it together, as a couple? Can we consider some ways we might give to others—ways to share from our happiness and from our material wealth? What a joy for us to live generously!

Dear God, teach us to live and to give with a generous spirit. Show us those who are in need and ways we can bless them with the abundance You've so graciously poured out onto us. Amen.

Quiet Moments

**Be still, and know that I am God;
I will be exalted among the nations,
I will be exalted in the earth!**

PSALM 46:10 NKJV

My Dear Wife,

I enjoy those peaceful moments. Does your spirit ever crave a haven of calm and peace? I know I sometimes want an undisturbed moment when I can just relax, knowing that God loves me. I think we need those times to experience God's grace all over again. And if we can do this outside in the midst of nature, enjoying God's beautiful creation, it's all the better. I'd love to share some of these quiet moments with you.

So, what do you think? Is this something you long for as well? How about if we spend some quiet time together, doing something we both enjoy, but without the need to fill up all the time and space with words or activities. Instead, let's just enjoy an undisturbed period of peaceful interlude—just you and me and God.

Dear God, show us some special ways to spend a quiet time together. Teach us to come to You consistently so we can experience Your peace and calm and be refreshed together. Amen.

We Both Change

**And as the Spirit of the Lord works within us,
we become more and more like him
and reflect his glory even more.**

2 CORINTHIANS 3:18 NLT

My Dear Wife,

I love what we're becoming. Just when we least expect it, change happens. It's inevitable. And as the years steadily move along, we can't help but change ourselves. To remain the same would be to become stagnant, to stop growing, perhaps to even die. And so with life pushing at us from all angles, we must change—we hope it's for the better. But some changes are hard to accept. Sometimes our human nature rebels against change. We want everything to remain constant and the same. But it doesn't.

So let's both try to accept that change really is good. And as we watch each other changing with the passing of years, let's applaud our milestones and celebrate these transitions, and let's welcome our new seasons of life with wide-open arms!

Dear God, You alone are changeless. Your love and grace and kindness remain constant throughout the ages. But we are in continual transition. We pray that You will change us to be more like You. Amen.

You and I Are One

The two will become one flesh.
So they are no longer two, but one.

MARK 10:8 NIV

~~~

$\mathcal{M}$y Dear Wife,

I bless you for our unity. I can't always completely comprehend what it means to be "one" with you. And yet, I know we're united in our marriage and in our love. But even so, we remain two very different and unique individuals. We maintain our very separate views, our separate personalities; we even have separate gifts and abilities. And yet I believe that God is making us one. It's really quite a wonderful mystery, one that continually astounds me with its dual complexity and simplicity.

While I know and respect that we are "separate" from each other, I am filled with enormous gratitude that our differences don't separate us— instead they make us stronger and truer to one another!

~~~

$\mathcal{D}$ear God, teach us to grow in respect for our differences and rejoice in respect to our "oneness." We are amazed by Your miraculous ability to take two people as different as we are and make us one. Amen.

When I Strive

Don't store up treasures here on earth, where they can be eaten by moths and get rusty. . . . Store your treasures in heaven.

MATTHEW 6:19-20 NLT

My Dear Wife,

I bless you for your values. Everyone seems to make a big deal about "success" these days. People talk about a "successful life" or "being successful." And I easily fall victim to this kind of thinking. After all, who doesn't want to succeed? Yet sometimes this focus makes me strive in the wrong areas, seeking money and prestige. To be honest, I know that's not how God defines real success.

I need to be reminded how to succeed for God—how to love Him and those around me better. I want to succeed at being a loving husband. I want to enjoy the simple everyday pleasures and appreciate the goodness of a life well lived. For I know that is far better than monetary success. And it's the only kind of success that's gratifying.

Dear God, help us to know what's really important in life. Teach us how to keep our focus on Your kind of success—the lasting kind. Show us ways we can encourage each other toward a better life in You. Amen.

What I Really Want

An excellent wife is the crown of her husband.

PROVERBS 12:4 NAS

My Dear Wife,

I love how you understand me. Sometimes I know you want to do something special—something you think will please me. And so maybe you try to do what you think I want you to do. The truth is that my greatest joy is being with you.

I would rather eat a simple meal with you than have you slaving over a fancy gourmet dinner that leaves you exhausted. And I'd rather spend time with you rather than have you rushing around making sure the house is all sparkling clean. Don't misunderstand me, sweetheart. I love everything you do, and it makes me feel good to know that you care so much to go to such lengths to make or do something special for me. Maybe we could even try cooking and cleaning together. That might be more fun than either of us could anticipate.

Dear God, we have so many daily responsibilities. Help us to do what we need to do and leave those things that aren't important, choosing instead the joy of being together. Amen.

What Would I Do without You?

**Has God forgotten to be gracious,
Or has He in anger withdrawn His compassion?**

PSALM 77:9 NAS

*M*y Dear Wife,

My life would be empty without you. I try to push such thoughts from my mind, for they bring discomfort and sadness. But occasionally, for just a split second, I have wondered what I would do if you were removed from my life. Where would I be if you were suddenly gone—taken in an instant? The answer feels so dismal that I can hardly stand to consider it.

My faith tells me that God would see me through such sadness. But, oh, how greatly I would miss all the little things you do, the times we enjoy together, and so very much. And because of that, I am more determined than ever to enjoy having you with me right now—to rejoice in each day that we have together—and to love you with everything that I've got.

---

*D*ear God, teach us to number our days on earth wisely. Help us to realize that any single one could be the last. And show us how to live fully, joyously, lovingly—and without remorse. Amen.

My Comfort Zone

Become complete. Be of good comfort, be of one mind,
live in peace; and the God of love and peace
will be with you.

2 CORINTHIANS 13:11 NKJV

My Dear Wife,

You are my place to come home to. Oh sure, I know people need to step out of their comfort zones occasionally. And although I usually appreciate that concept, there is one area where I must personally resist. And that's because you are my comfort zone, and no one is going to persuade to step away from you!

Because I love being around you! I love taking you into my arms, and I love experiencing your love. And I also love taking care of you and protecting you. And I believe that's why God gave you to me, specifically, to be my comfort zone. I hope I am the same for you. I hope when you step into my presence you feel at home, cherished, loved, safe. Let's never leave these comfort zones, my love!

Dear God, thank You for the comfort and security of our marriage. We know that a good marriage is a gift from You. Amen.

Let's Create a Moment

I am about to do a brand-new thing. See, I have already begun!

ISAIAH 43:19 NLT

❧

My Dear Wife,

I love making new "firsts" with you. With fondness, I remember the first time we met. I recall our first date; and that first time I took you into my arms. And, oh, do I remember that first sweet kiss! And I wonder if we can make another kind of "first time" moment together. Is it possible to create something new together again? Or maybe we can do something old in a brand new way. However we do it, I want to make a new memory with you!

Shall we plan a little getaway—an excursion for just the two of us? Or maybe we could get up really early and watch the sun rise over the eastern horizon. Let's dream up something goofy and unexpected. Whatever it is, we can create something fresh and new—something we can both enjoy and remember for a long, long time.

❧

Dear God, help us to break out of our routine and enjoy a special moment that is all new. Thank You for inspiring us with Your mercies that are new every morning. Amen.

My Favorite Things

Then he crowns it all with green, lush pastures in the wilderness; hillsides blossom with joy. The pastures are filled with flocks of sheep, and the valleys are carpeted with grain. All the world shouts with joy and sings.

PSALM 65:11-13 TLB

My Dear Wife,

I bless you for sweet simplicity. It's really the simple things that bring me the most joy, my love. Just those everyday pleasures that happen when you live life fully and well. You don't have to cook French cuisine, dress in silk, or get your hair done to push my romantic buttons. Not that those things aren't nice, but my favorite things are a lot easier to come by.

Let's try things like snuggling together in bed for an extra few minutes before we both head off to our busy days, or holding hands in a crowd of strangers. There are so many possibilities, like sharing an intimate conversation for two or walking together beneath a canopy of stars. You see, all my favorite things include you.

Dear God, as we spend simple moments together, we want to honor Your presence in our lives as well. Thank You for all the beauty and grandeur in our world and the simple joy of being in love. Amen.

The Way You Walk

My beloved responded and said to me,
"Arise, my darling, my beautiful one,
And come along.
For behold, the winter is past,
The rain is over and gone."

SONG OF SOLOMON 2:10-11 NAS

My Dear Wife,

You have a walk like no other. We can be separated in crowded mall, and if I'm watching, even from a distance, I can usually spot you. For you have this certain, unmistakable stride that belongs to no one but you. And it's just one of those many unique characteristics that I so love about you. I'm so thankful that God made you just the way He did.

And your sweet smile is no different—it's that light-up-a-room and light-up-my-heart kind of smile. And then there's the way your eyes twinkle when you're happy, or the way you giggle at my jokes, or how you hold your head at a certain angle when you're thinking. All these special traits are undeniably you. And how I love each and every one!

Dear God, thank You for the unique qualities You place in each person. It makes living so much more interesting and fun. Amen.

Our Favorite Song

We praise you, LORD, for all your glorious power.
With music and singing we celebrate
your mighty acts.

PSALM 21:13 NLT

*M*y Dear Wife,

You are like sweet music to me. Doesn't every couple have a special song? Perhaps it's a favorite tune that was popular when they first courted, something that was performed at their wedding, or just some song that holds some special meaning for both of them. What is ours, my love? Do we have one? Let's remember the songs we used to enjoy together. Let's listen to them again, and let's remember why they meant so much back then. Or consider what they mean to us now.

And if we can't remember a specific song, then let's put our heads together and come up with a brand-new song. And let's make it our own special song—a milestone of the time we've spent together, a reminder of our ongoing romance, a small token of our love.

*D*ear God, music is a gift from You and it stirs up deep emotions. We pray that our lives would be music to Your ears. Amen.

You're My Soul Mate

I am overcome with joy because of your unfailing love,
for you have seen my troubles,
and you care about the anguish of my soul.
You have not handed me over to my enemy
but have set me in a safe place.

PSALM 31:7 NLT

*M*y Dear Wife,

I bless you for your kindred heart. For me to fully appreciate the importance of a soul mate, I need to better understand what our souls consist of. And I believe our souls are that inner place where we can appreciate the beauty of nature, or enjoy a well-told tale or a really good song. And I thank God for giving each of us a unique soul.

But if we're meant to be soul mates, my love, we need to share some of these same soulful pleasures together. Maybe it's as simple as admiring a lovely sunset, or as complex as understanding an old piece of classical literature. But whatever it is that gives our souls pleasure, let's take time to experience these things together.

---

*D*ear God, all of the earthly pleasures of music, literature, art, and nature are part of Your great creation. As we experience these great gifts, we thank You for Your awesome goodness to us. Amen.

When I Blow It

Your heavenly Father will forgive you if you forgive those who sin against you; but if you refuse to forgive them, he will not forgive you.

MATTHEW 6:14-15 TLB

*M*y Dear Wife,

I bless you for your gracious spirit. Just like almost everyone, I wish I were perfect. But we both know I'm not even close. You, more than anyone, have seen, close up, how human I am. Whether it stems from selfishness, pride, or just basic ignorance, the truth is I can blow it big time. And it feels lousy when I do.

But you know what makes the biggest difference in the world? It's the way you react when I behave badly. When you're gracious and kind and forgiving and supportive, I feel like I can pick myself up and go on. I will always appreciate Your forgiving spirit that looks past my faults and failings.

---

*D*ear God, help us both to be quick to support the other when we blow it. Teach us to be gracious and forgiving. Show us how to lend a hand to help the other one up. Amen.

What We're Building

Unless the Lord builds the house,
They labor in vain who build it;
Unless the Lord guards the city,
The watchman keeps awake in vain.

PSALM 127:1 NAS

My Dear Wife,

I love what we are becoming. I'm proud of what we are building together—our love, our home, and our family. I know I can get so caught up in the pressures of work or the demands of daily living that I almost forget that you and I are working on something important and big—something significant. And something lasting.

I want our marriage, our family, our home to be like a city on a high hill—something that people can see from miles around and that will make them marvel. I want our love to shine like a beacon of hope to those who witness it, reminding them that God is good and grace is real. And I want to build something that will continue even after we are gone.

Dear God, we need Your help to build this thing. We need Your hands on our lives to make our marriage a monument to You—a symbol of Your love, Your grace, Your mercy, Your forgiveness. Amen.

I Remember When . . .

I remember what the LORD did;
I remember the miracles you did long ago.
I think about all the things you did
and consider your deeds.

PSALM 77:11-12 NCV

*M*y Dear Wife,

I bless you for all our days. Do you recall that first time when our eyes met? Tell me I didn't imagine that unforgettable look that told me "something's going on here." Or what about that incredible rush that ran through me? Surely I wasn't the only one who felt the electricity in the air? And I remember the first time I wrapped my hand around yours and felt the warmth of your smooth fingers. You will always be safe in my arms.

I recall the first time I wiped away your tears, how I held you close and tried to wrap you up in a blanket of my love. And I remember the time you did the same for me. We've been through a lot together. All those experiences, so many memories. Maybe we can take time to remember them together—and celebrate them again.

*D*ear God, thank You for bringing us so far and keeping our love strong and vibrant. We feel Your blessing on our marriage each day. Amen.

Planning Romance

*So I decided it was more important to enjoy life. The best that
people can do here on earth is eat, drink, and enjoy life, because
these joys will help them do the hard work
God gives them here on earth.*

ECCLESIASTES 8:15 NCV

&

My Dear Wife,

*I love that you take time for romance. Remember when we were young
and head over heels in love, and it seemed that romance just happened all on
its own? It didn't seem like we went to much trouble; being together was
enough. Sometimes you were all I could think about as we pursued our
times together—times to walk and talk and laugh and share.*

*But things change, and life's more complicated now than it used to be.
And suddenly it makes sense to plan for romance. I see the need to schedule
a date or make preparations for some romantic ambiance. And just because
these moments don't "just happen" doesn't mean they're any less meaningful.
In fact, I think I appreciate them more than ever now.*

*Dear God, help us to be diligent to plan time with You as well as with
each other—time to talk and listen and renew our commitment to You.
Amen.*

Let's Talk about Eternity

Love never fails. But where there are prophecies, they will cease; where there are tongues, they will be stilled; where there is knowledge, it will pass away.

1 CORINTHIANS 13:8 NIV

My Dear Wife,

Our hearts together, forever. Do we really understand what this means? I'm afraid our earthbound minds cannot fully understand the concept of forever and eternity very well. For only God can comprehend these things. And do you ever wonder what it will be like when we are parted by death? What will happen to our love then?

That's when I realize I must simply trust God with such things. I need to remember that He's the One who bound our hearts together, and only He knows what will happen to us in eternity. But I do know this, our love will continue in some shape or form. Because a love as real as this surely cannot die.

Dear God, some things are too great for our human, finite minds to understand—things like what will happen to our relationship when there's no such thing as marriage in Heaven. But we know we can trust You with these questions. And like little children, we know You know best. Amen

Our Love Complete

Christ's love is greater than anyone can ever know, but I pray that you will be able to know that love.

EPHESIANS 3:19 NCV

My Dear Wife,

I bless you for allowing God to love through you. Even if I tried to love you with everything that I have within me, it wouldn't be a complete and perfect love. For, after all, I'm only human. Though sincere, my love often falls short, missing the mark—or it stops too soon. But I do believe God can complete my love. He can empower me to go the extra mile and to love you selflessly and completely.

I want to allow God to love through me like this. I want to become all that I can be in our marriage—to be more loving and kind, more generous and caring. But I know it will take time and commitment, and most of all God, before my love for you is complete.

Dear God, You've begun a good work in our marriage, You've planted Your seeds of love in our hearts. But we realize that only You can bring our love to a place of completion. And we know it's a lifelong process. We pray that You'll help us to cooperate with Your plan. Amen.

A Shared Vision

*Ask me and I will tell you some remarkable secrets
about what is going to happen here.*

JEREMIAH 33:3 TLB

❦

*M*y Dear Wife,

*I love when our hearts are united in purpose. With time, I know our
love will grow and our relationship will deepen. But I also hope we can
begin to share a bigger vision for what God might have us do. For perhaps
He has united us for a special reason, something that's beyond our own
personal fulfillment and delight. And I look forward to serving God, side
by side, with you in some unique way.*

*I want God to bless our relationship that we might touch others. I want
our marriage to become an outreach of love and kindness to those around
us. For when our cup is so full, how can we hold back the abundance of
blessings? How can we keep all God's grace and goodness to ourselves? And
as we give and share, we will also be blessed.*

❦

*D*ear God, we pray You'll give us a clear vision of what You'd like to
do in our lives. Show us ways You can bless others through our relationship.
Pour Yourself through us and onto others. Amen.

Together Forever

Surely goodness and mercy shall follow me
All the days of my life;
And I will dwell in the house of the LORD.
Forever.

PSALM 23:6 NKJV

My Dear Wife,

I will love you always. How can we possibly understand the complexities of what our relationship will become when we step into the next life? But as we enter our amazing heavenly home, I want to believe we'll be there together. And how could it be that you, my wife, my closest earthly friend, would not stand next to me with your hand in mine.

I hope I can be by your side as we look up in incredulous wonder at those majestic heavenly gates. And I want to walk with you as we worship the King of all kings. Things will be different in Heaven; I'm sure of that. But I firmly believe our union will remain as strong—yes, even stronger—than it has been on earth.

Dear God, thank You for this wonderful bond You have created in the earth—this miracle called marriage. As we continue to walk through this life together, we pray that You would continue to bless our union. And for that, we give You all the glory. Amen.